...IF YOUR NAME WAS CHANGED
at Ellis Island

by Ellen Levine
illustrated by Wayne Parmenter

SCHOLASTIC INC.
New York   Toronto   London   Auckland   Sydney

In memory of my grandfather Louis Nachimovsky, whose name was changed at Ellis Island; and for everyone else in my family who passed through the Great Hall.

In gratitude to all the immigrants who passed through Ellis Island and contributed their memories and artifacts to make the museum an historical treasure trove.

I am particularly grateful to Paul Sigrist, Oral Historian of the Ellis Island Museum, who most generously shared his knowledge and his files with me.

ISBN 0-590-43829-8
ISBN 0-590-29100-9 (meets NASTA specifications)

Text copyright © 1993 by Ellen Levine.
Illustrations copyright © 1993 by Scholastic Inc.
All rights reserved. Published by Scholastic Inc.

1 2 3 4 5 6 7 8 9 10   08   00 99 98 97 96 95 94 93

Printed in the U.S.A.

Book design by Laurie McBarnette
The illustrations in this book were painted in acrylic on illustration board.

CONTENTS

Introduction

America has always been a nation of immigrants — people who have moved to the United States from other countries. Even the first Americans, the Indians, are believed to have crossed the Bering Strait over a strip of land that once connected North America with Asia thousands and thousands of years ago.

When the thirteen colonies were first settled, most immigrants came from England, Holland, and France. Soon there were Scandinavians, Welsh, Scots, Scotch-Irish, Irish, and Germans. As early as 1643, a French priest visiting New Amsterdam, which later became New York City, said that eighteen different languages could be heard spoken in the city streets.

By the end of the 1800s, Italians, Poles, Armenians, Russians, and others from southern and eastern Europe began to pour into America. On the west coast, Chinese and Japanese immigrants arrived.

It was the greatest human migration in history. We don't really know exactly how many people came, because for long periods of time no records were kept. And when they were, only some people were counted, not others. We do know that nearly 35 million people came to America in the one hundred years from the 1820s until 1924. In that year, strict immigration laws were passed to limit the number of people who could enter the country.

For most of the newcomers, the trip was difficult, often dangerous. They traveled weeks, sometimes months, only to arrive in a place where they didn't speak the language. Often they had nowhere to live and little money. Yet they poured into America.

This book is about their journey, their hopes and difficulties, and their adventures. It tells the stories mainly of those immigrants who came through New York Harbor from the 1880s until 1914, when World War I began and the great migrations ended.

For these immigrants, America was their destination, Ellis Island the first stop.

What was Ellis Island?

Ellis Island was an immigration center located in New York Harbor. Millions of newcomers passed through its gates and were examined by doctors and legal inspectors. Some were allowed to enter the United States right away, some were detained (held for a while), and some were deported (rejected and sent back).

Before Ellis Island opened, immigrants had been examined at Castle Garden at the tip of Manhattan Island. At one time Castle Garden had been a fort, then a concert hall. In 1855 it was turned into an immigration center. Thirty-five years later, it was no longer big enough to handle the thousands of new immigrants arriving daily.

The U.S. government then decided to use a small piece of land in New York Harbor known as Ellis Island for a new immigration center. The Ellis Island station opened in 1892. During the next thirty years, more people came to America than at any other time. At least 12 million of them passed through Ellis Island.

Did all immigrants come through Ellis Island?

Most immigrants to America came through Ellis Island, but not all. Some entered through other east coast ports in Boston, Philadelphia, or Baltimore; southern or southwestern ports like New Orleans and Galveston; or west coast cities like San Francisco. In 1907, the year when more immigrants came to the United States than at any other time, there were seventy immigration stations. But ninety percent of all the newcomers at that time passed through Ellis Island.

Not all immigrants who arrived in New York had to go through Ellis Island. If you had the most expensive tickets on the ship — first or second class — immigration inspectors examined you while you were aboard the ship in the harbor. If you passed the inspection, you were free to enter the country when the boat docked in New York. Only the poor who traveled in third class or steerage — the cheapest way to travel — were taken to Ellis Island.

Why did people leave their homelands?

Some people left because of a catastrophe like an earthquake or famine. In Ireland, for example, a terrible disease in the mid-1800s destroyed the main farm crop — potatoes — for several years in a row. The famine lasted many years, and nearly 2 million people died of starvation. Almost as many people left for America. When there was a famine in Sweden in the 1860s, whole villages packed up and came to America.

Millions of immigrants fled for other reasons. In the late 1800s and early 1900s, thousands of Russian Jews were killed in terrible pogroms, which were massacres often organized by the government and sometimes even by churches. More than 2 million Jews left Russia and eastern Europe because of these pogroms, as well as other kinds of religious persecution.

Thousands of people fled their country for other reasons. Many left to avoid being rounded up into their government's army and forced to serve for many years. Others, who had fought to overthrow their country's dictator, lost, and then had to flee. Some left because of sickness at home. A deadly flu epidemic in Turkey, for example, drove many people from their homes.

Most people left because they couldn't earn a living in their country. Newly invented factory machines replaced many workers. New farm techniques and machinery also put many small farmers out of work. As people flocked from the countryside to the cities, they lived in crowded and poor conditions. They left for America, hoping to find work and a better life.

Why did people come to America?

Many people believed that America was a "Golden Land" — a place where you could get a decent job, go to a free school, and eat well. There was a saying in Polish that people came to America *za chlebem* — "for bread." One person added that they came "for bread, with butter."

In Russia, six-year-old Alec Bodanis was told that in America, "you'll become a millionaire in no time. Take a shovel with you because they shovel gold from the streets." No one knows how these stories began, but Margot Matyshek, age eleven when she left Germany, had also heard that in America, "the streets are paved with gold. And if you wish for candy, it drops from the sky right into your mouth!"

Some people came to look for work. Wages were higher in America than in their home countries. Until the late 1800s, businesses often sent agents overseas to encourage workers to migrate. If you agreed to work for their companies, they would pay your way to America.

Many people came because land was cheap and plentiful. In 1862, the U.S. government passed a law called the Homestead Act. Newcomers could stake a claim to 160 acres of land. After five years of living on and working the land, they'd pay a small amount of money, and the acres would be theirs. Railroad companies also owned a great deal of land in the west. They sent agents to foreign countries offering this land for sale at good prices.

Some governments of the new western states advertised in European newspapers about their growing towns and cheap farmland. They wanted new settlers. Often the advertisements were not true. They showed pictures of towns that didn't exist, and gave descriptions of farm fields where forests stood. But people came anyway. Searching, always searching, for a better life.

A Swedish song had these words about America:

"Ducks and chickens rain right down,
A roasted goose flies in,
And on the table lands one more
with knife and fork stuck in."

Who could find a better place?

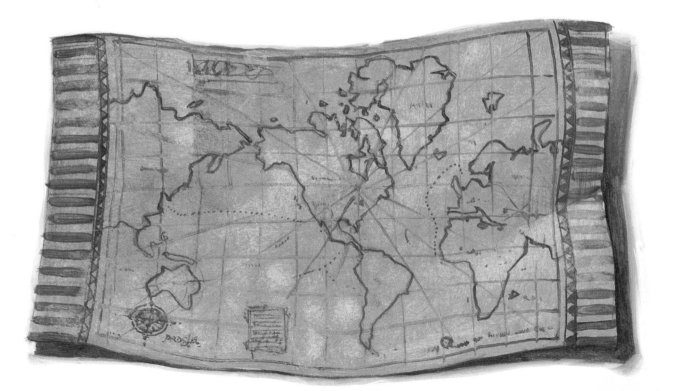

Did every immigrant come voluntarily?

No. In 1619, a year before the pilgrims landed at Plymouth Rock, the first shipload of twenty black slaves arrived at Jamestown, Virginia. For more than two hundred years, slaves were kidnapped from Africa and sold in America. They were immigrants, but they didn't come of their own free will.

But not all blacks came as slaves. Some came by choice, usually from different Caribbean islands. They came for the same reasons most people did — to make a better life.

Would everyone in your family come together?

Most families did not come together. Often a father or an older brother or sister would come first. That person would find work and send money back to "the old country" to bring the others over. For most families it took at least a year to be reunited; for others, ten or more years. If you were very young when, say, your father left, you might not even recognize him when you finally arrived in America.

Sometimes your relative or friend in America made arrangements with a bank or railroad or steamship company agent to send you the tickets and money for your trip. Then you would have to get to the seaport where your ship sailed from.

What did people bring with them?

Usually whatever they could carry. Some had suitcases and trunks. Most had bundles tied together with string. People carried baskets, cardboard boxes, tins, leather sacks — any type of container you could imagine.

They often brought their feather quilts, mattresses, and pillows, for the steamships just provided thin blankets. They packed fancy clothes, specially embroidered and crocheted. Sometimes people wore layers of all their clothing so they wouldn't have to pack them. Often they brought food for the long trip over the ocean, like smoked sausages or hams, or other foods they thought they couldn't get in America.

Many people had to sell or give away almost everything they owned in order to travel to the new land. But sometimes they were able to bring their favorite things. One young girl mailed her dolls to her relatives in America before she herself came. Another brought a book of fairy tales, which she carried in a basket she held tightly for the whole trip.

How did people travel to the ships that brought them to America?

There were many different ways people reached the port cities.

If you lived out in the country, you often had to go to a big town to catch a train to the port. When some families left, everyone came to say good-bye. In one village the band played as the family rode off. Other people, many from Russia or Poland, left their towns in the dead of night to escape mobs that were beating and murdering people.

There were many difficulties you might face before you reached the ship. Oftentimes you would have to cross the border into another country before you reached the port. To do that you might need a special permit, but permits were usually difficult to get. Sometimes the government of your country didn't want boys and young men to leave. They wanted them to serve in the army.

You might face other problems. Thieves frequently stole your goods when you stayed at inns or slept in fields. And if you reached a border and didn't have a permit, you might have to pay a bribe to the border guard to allow you to cross.

The trip overland sometimes took weeks. One family had to reach the port of Istanbul to board their ship. But they were stuck in a town on the Black Sea for a year because of a local war.

Finally when you arrived at a port city, you might have to wait a week or two, sometimes even longer, until the ship was ready to depart.

Were you examined before you left?

According to a U.S. law, ship companies had to pay the return fare for anyone who had to be sent back from America. And so before leaving, ship doctors examined all passengers to see if they had any illnesses that would prevent them from being allowed to enter the United States. The doctors vaccinated and disinfected all passengers. Men and boys often had their hair cut very short, and women and girls had theirs combed very carefully to look for lice, which carried the deadly disease typhus.

The ship companies also had to prepare a manifest — a list of information about everybody on board the ship. Each immigrant was assigned a number, and the ship's captain listed everyone's nationality, age, sex, destination, and occupation. Travelers were asked if they could read and write, whether they were married, and how many pieces of baggage they had. This list was given to the immigration inspectors when the ship landed in America.

How long would the ocean trip take?

Until the mid-1800s, most people came to America on sailing ships. These usually took about forty days to cross the Atlantic Ocean, but sometimes it could take up to six months. By the late 1800s, steamships had replaced sailing ships, and the trip was much faster. If there were no bad storms or other problems, the trip usually took anywhere from six to thirty-two days.

Where would you sleep and eat on the ship?

If you traveled first or second class, you would have a private cabin to sleep in, and food would be served in a dining room. But most immigrants traveled in the least-expensive way — in steerage.

The steerage area was below the deck, on the lowest level of the ship. Several hundred passengers were crammed into steerage with no fresh air. They slept in narrow bunk beds, sometimes three high. When one seven-year-old came from Barbados in January, she and the other passengers were so cold on board that many were frostbitten.

Usually there was one bath area for all the steerage passengers, with sink faucets that frequently didn't work. Immigrants often talked about the filth in the steerage area.

The food for steerage passengers wasn't much better than their sleeping areas. Lukewarm soup, boiled potatoes, and stringy beef were often the only items on the menu.

Many immigrants reported that all they ate was herring, bread, potatoes, and tea. The one good thing about so much herring, some said, was that it helped prevent seasickness.

One reporter, who wanted to see what it was like to travel in steerage, boarded a ship in Naples in 1906. When he arrived in America, he wrote:

"How can a steerage passenger remember that he is a human being when he must first pick the worms from his food . . . and eat in his stuffy, stinking bunk, or in the hot . . . atmosphere of a compartment where 150 men sleep?"

What would you do all day?

If the weather was good, you would spend as much time as possible on deck and out of the steerage area. Some kids played marbles or dominoes. Others helped sailors with chores. Sometimes there were religious services.

One young boy said that if the day was clear, the women would go up on the deck and wash the children's hair. His mother had told him they'd all be sent back home if the American immigration inspectors found lice.

Children frequently had the best time of anyone on board. They'd wander around the ship listening to all the different languages, sometimes learning a few words in English.

Was the ocean voyage dangerous?

Shipwrecks, sickness, and fires were the main worries. Karl Raffe was on a ship in 1892 when a fierce storm began to rage. "Many people started to vomit," he wrote in his diary. "I also got very dizzy! . . . So far as your eyes can see is nothing but high waves and a whole ocean in an uproar. In the night a little baby was born. Through all the motion of the ship it came too soon."

Surviving storms was sometimes easier than surviving sickness on board. On one ship all the children came down with measles. Some died and were buried at sea.

In the mid-1800s, ship conditions were so crowded and unsanitary that diseases spread rapidly. Thousands died from typhus, called "ship fever," and cholera. So many people died from these diseases that some newspapers called the ships "swimming coffins."

By the end of the 1800s, most people were traveling by steamship. These ships were larger, made of iron, then steel, and were less damaged by storms and fires. In addition, the conditions, particularly in steerage, were crowded but not as bad as in earlier years. There were still outbreaks of disease, but every ship had a doctor on board and ways of separating sick passengers from everyone else.

Would you go straight to Ellis Island when you arrived in New York Harbor?

When a ship arrived in New York Harbor, immigrants crowded the decks to look at the tall buildings, the "mountains of New York" as some called them. Greeting the newcomers was the Statue of Liberty, rising, it seemed, right out of the water. Some thought it was a statue of Christopher Columbus. Others knew it as the "Lady Liberty" who welcomed immigrants to the new world. Everyone knew it meant they had finally arrived.

All the ships were stopped in lower New York bay, where doctors boarded. They checked passengers for contagious diseases, like typhus, yellow fever, small-pox, and cholera. There were two small islands in the lower bay. If you were sick, you'd be put in a hospital on one of them. If the doctors thought you had been exposed to a disease, they'd place you on the other island for observation. In later years Ellis Island itself had a hospital for people with contagious diseases.

A little further up the bay, immigration officers examined all the first- and second-class passengers. Then the boat would dock at the tip of Manhattan Island, and those passengers who had passed inspection would get off, free to enter the country.

Steerage passengers, however, had to go to Ellis Island. Frequently, they stayed on board ship for one or more nights until barges could take them over to Ellis Island for further examination. One nineteen-year-old immigrant said, as he watched the first- and second-class passengers leave the ship:

"Isn't it strange that here we are coming to a country where there is complete equality, but not quite so for the newly arrived immigrants."

Where would you go when you landed at Ellis Island?

When the barge pulled up to the dock at Ellis Island, immigrants walked under the entry arches into the ground-floor baggage room where some left their luggage. Others held on to all their bags. One baggage worker said he could recognize what country people had come from by the type of luggage they carried and by the way they tied the knots around their bundles.

Then they went up a staircase into the Registry Room, also known as the Great Hall. There they would be examined again by doctors and then by immigration inspectors.

As they reached the top of the stairs, the Great Hall spread out before them like a huge maze. Metal pipes divided the space into narrow aisles, and sections were enclosed in wire mesh. One young immigrant said, "You think you're in a zoo!" After 1911, the iron pipes were removed and replaced by long rows of wooden benches.

Hundreds, at times thousands, of immigrants passed through the Great Hall. The noise, some said, was like the Tower of Babel — sometimes thirty languages being spoken at the same time.

Ellis Island was like a miniature city for immigrants. There were waiting rooms, dormitories for over a thousand people, restaurants, a hospital, baggage room, post office, banks to change foreign money, a railroad ticket office, medical and legal examination rooms, baths, laundries, office areas for charities and church groups, and courtrooms.

Ellis Island was the last hurdle you had to pass before you were to enter the country.

Who examined you at Ellis Island?

Doctors were the first to examine you, and they began before you even knew it. When you walked up the stairs to the Great Hall, doctors were watching you. They wanted to see if you limped or had any difficulty breathing. When you reached the top, they looked at your skin, throat, hands, and scalp. Children older than two had to walk by themselves. All immigrants were asked their names to see if they could hear and speak.

Other doctors used a finger or a metal buttonhook to roll your eyelids back to see if you had a very contagious eye disease called trachoma. One little girl was almost sent back home because her eyes were all red. She had been sick on board ship, and had cried so much that her eyes were sore. After three days of rest, she was allowed to stay.

The walk up the stairs was called the "six-second medical," and then the doctors at the top usually took two to three minutes to examine you. All of these exams together usually took less than five minutes.

What happened if the doctors found something wrong with you?

If the doctors thought something was wrong, they would put a chalk mark on your clothes at your shoulder or back. An "X" stood for a possible mental problem. "B" for back. "E" for eyes. "P" for physical or lungs. "Sc" for scalp. "L" for lameness. "CT" for trachoma. Every child's head and nails were examined for lice and a contagious disease called favus.

If you had a chalk mark, you'd have to go for further examinations. One young girl, nervous about leaving her home and coming to a new country, had developed warts on her hands. The doctor chalked an "X" on her coat. She and her family were very afraid that she might be sent back home. She was wearing a new coat with a very pretty lining. A kind man told her to turn her coat inside out so that the chalk mark wouldn't show. She never found out if he was an inspector or another immigrant. But she did what he suggested and was not examined again.

If you were detained, you were taken to a special area for further examination. If your sickness was curable, you were kept in the hospital until you were better. Many babies and young people arrived with measles, scarlet fever, or diphtheria. Favus, a scalp and nail disease, was also common. Most children stayed in the hospital one to two weeks before they were released. To keep diseases from spreading, there was a printed warning for the nurses on the wall of the children's wards: "Do not kiss a patient."

If your disease was contagious and incurable, you were put in a special hospital area until a steamship took you back to the seaport city you had come from.

What kinds of mental tests were you given?

If the doctors wanted to give you an intelligence test, they'd mark you with an "X." They wanted to be certain that you were not "feebleminded." If you were a child, they wanted to be certain that when you grew up you'd be able to work.

When you were marked with an "X," you were taken to a special room where they would ask you a few questions about yourself. Ellis Island had to have interpreters for at least thirty different languages. The examiners would give you some simple arithmetic problems, ask you to count backwards from twenty to one, and have you complete a puzzle.

In one test you would put wooden pieces of different shapes into a pegboard. You might be asked to read a paragraph. If you didn't know how to read, you'd be shown pictures of eight faces and asked to pick the four happy or unhappy ones. You'd then be asked to match up similar drawings from two groups of pictures.

One young girl had an "X" chalked on her shoulder. When she passed all the tests easily, the doctors said, "Oh, we must have made a mistake." And then they removed the "X."

Sometimes you were asked to explain the meaning of a picture. In one drawing a group of American children was watching a boy dig a hole in a garden. A dead rabbit was lying on the ground near the boy. Many immigrants said that the children had killed the rabbit for dinner, a common practice in Europe. The answer the doctors expected was that they were burying a pet that had died.

Fiorello La Guardia was mayor of New York City for many years. But before he became mayor, he worked as an interpreter on Ellis Island. He believed that more than half of the people who were sent home because of supposed mental problems should have been allowed to stay. He said that the Ellis Island doctors often didn't understand that people from other countries might do things and think about things differently from Americans. Instead, the doctors would decide that the immigrants had mental problems, and send them home. La Guardia thought that was wrong.

What did the legal inspectors do?

After you were cleared by the doctors, you would wait in long aisles until your ship number, called a manifest number, was called. Then you would move up the aisles, slowly, with all the people from your ship. Everyone had an identification card with the manifest number on it. Many people wore their ID cards around their necks or pinned to their clothing.

The legal inspectors sat at high desks at the end of the Great Hall. Next to them were interpreters. Each inspector had the ship's list — the manifest — that the officers had filled out with information about every passenger. The inspectors had to decide whether you were, in the words of the law, "clearly and beyond a doubt entitled to land."

They asked each immigrant between twenty and thirty questions. They wanted to know your name, place of birth, where you were coming from and where you were going, if you had any relatives in

America, who paid for your passage, and other such questions. The inspectors had so many people to examine that they usually spent only two to three minutes with each person.

Although most immigrants passed the legal examination, it was often very confusing and frightening for people. Questions were shot at them like bullets from a gun. The interpreters weren't always very accurate. And most of all, every immigrant knew that a "wrong" answer, or an answer the inspector didn't like, could mean you would be deported — sent back to your old homeland.

Did you have to have any money when you arrived?

The United States immigration law said that a person could not come into the country if he or she would become a "public charge." That meant the government did not want to have to pay money to house, clothe, or feed people. And so the Commissioner of Immigration made a rule that everyone entering the country had to have ten dollars and money for railroad tickets. Later the amount was raised to twenty-five dollars.

Twenty-five dollars was a lot of money for many immigrants. People often had to work months to save that much. Immigrant aid groups in America challenged the rule in a court case and won. But even though the rule was dropped, many inspectors continued to use it.

Immigrants often helped one another. After they passed inspection, they would secretly hand the money down the line to those behind them. Others were helped by ships' officers. Since the steamship companies had to pay for your return trip if you were not admitted to America, some ships' officers lent immigrants money until they had passed through the inspection. But as soon as they passed, the immigrants had to pay it back.

If you didn't have enough money with you, you were often detained for days until a relative or friend sent the money to you at Ellis Island.

Did you have to have a job waiting for you?

No, and if you did, you could be in trouble. You might be sent back to your old homeland. In 1885 the U.S. Congress passed a law that said employers could not make contracts — agreements — with immigrants to bring them to America, promising them jobs. Congress was afraid that immigrants would accept lower wages than American workers, and so take jobs away from those already living here.

This presented a real problem for immigrants. On the one hand, they couldn't have a job waiting for them. On the other, they had to show that they were able and willing to work, and wouldn't have any problem getting a job. If you couldn't support yourself, you could become a "public charge." Then the government could send you back to your old country.

Did you have to be able to read English?

Most of the immigrants who came through Ellis Island were not asked if they could read. Then in 1917 Congress passed a law saying that anyone over age sixteen had to be able to read. You didn't have to read English. You just had to be able to read some language.

Those who supported the law didn't want so many people coming to the United States from southern and eastern Europe. Some thought that these immigrants were inferior to those who had come from England, Germany, and Scandinavia. Others were afraid that Americans would lose jobs to the immigrants because the newcomers would be willing to work for less money. By making immigrants pass a literacy test, they hoped to keep many people out.

Once the literacy law was passed, immigration inspectors had cards printed in different languages — Hindustani, Persian, Romanian, Hebrew, German, Russian, Greek, Armenian, Turkish, Polish, Swedish, Italian, etc. Each card had a forty-word passage that the immigrant had to read.

One young Armenian girl was very afraid that her mother would be deported because she couldn't read. But the woman was very lucky. The inspector who examined her was a kind man. Perhaps he believed that she would make a good citizen even though she couldn't read. He knew she was religious and could recite the Lord's Prayer. So he handed her a page that had the prayer printed in Armenian, and told her to read. She then "read" it, and passed.

What happened if you were detained?

If you were detained because you were sick, you'd be put in the hospital and treated until you were better. If your disease was incurable or contagious, you were deported. Trachoma, the contagious eye disease that led to blindness, was the most common medical reason people were deported.

You would also be deported if the inspectors thought you

— had committed crimes in the old country;

— or had come to America with the promise of a job;

— or wouldn't be able to support yourself or your family;

— or had certain mental or physical problems that would keep you from being able to work.

Then you would get a chalk mark, "SI," or a tag that said "Special Inquiry." You'd wait until three inspectors with an interpreter would hear your case. It was like a court of law, but you weren't allowed to have a lawyer speak for you. If this Board of Special Inquiry ruled against you, you could appeal all the way to the officials in charge of immigration in Washington, D.C.

About twenty of every hundred immigrants went before a Board of Special Inquiry. But only about two of every hundred were deported. That sounds like a low number, but in some years thousands of immigrants were coming every day. That would mean more than a thousand were turned away every month.

How long would you stay at Ellis Island?

Most people were questioned, examined, and ready to leave the island after three to five hours. Some had to stay much longer.

Lillian Kaiz and her brother both came down with the measles, and their mother caught pneumonia. They were kept in separate wards of the hospital. Three weeks passed before they were well enough to leave the island.

If you didn't have much money with you, you needed a sponsor, a person who said they'd be responsible for supporting you until you found work. Sometimes you would be detained until the sponsor or necessary money arrived.

Some people were denied entry and had to go back to their old homes. Families then had to make a painful decision: should everyone return, or should the family break up? Any child who was sent back had to be accompanied by an adult.

What would you eat at Ellis Island?

If you were detained, or arrived at night and couldn't be processed until the next day, you were served meals in the Ellis Island restaurant.

There were two kitchens, one regular and one kosher for religious Jews. In the dining room you sat at long wooden tables. For breakfast you might be

served eggs, bread, butter, coffee, or milk. A typical dinner or supper included soup, beef stew, vegetables, potatoes, pudding, coffee, milk, and sometimes a piece of fruit.

Some of the food was strange and different for the immigrants. One young girl remembered the first time she ate a banana. She had never seen one before, and neither had any of the people she was with. One person ate the banana, skin and all, before they all were told to peel it.

An eleven-year-old boy remembered that "every night they gave us two or three cookies, fig bars, and a glass of milk. I never tasted that before in my life. They were good!"

The steamship company that brought you to America paid for your food and care while you were on Ellis Island. But if you were traveling farther than New York City, you had to pay for your own box lunch.

Where would you sleep?

If you stayed overnight at Ellis Island, you'd sleep either in the hospital or in a dormitory. During the years of the greatest migration to America, both were usually overcrowded. In the dorms there were long rows of triple-decker bunks separated by narrow aisles. Men and women slept in separate areas. Children were usually with their mothers.

Was there anything to do while you waited?

Most of the time people waited, nervously, to pass through the next stage of the inspection. If you were detained, you might wait for days or weeks before you could leave the island.

For many years there were no activities for those who were detained. They were only allowed outdoors on the rooftop where there was an exercise area. There was also a playground for kids on the roof, with a tricycle, cart, rocking horse, and many flags.

In 1914 Frederic C. Howe became Commissioner of Immigration at Ellis Island. He was called a re-former, and he made many changes. He let the immigrants use the lawns as play areas if the weather was good. He also set up a kindergarten for young children, set aside meeting rooms for adults, and arranged for concerts, movies, training classes, and athletic games.

What was the Staircase of Separation?

At the end of the Great Hall was the Staircase of Separation. Whether you passed all the examinations or were detained, you went down that staircase. A turn to the right at the bottom led to the railroad ticket office. A turn to the left led to the ferry to Manhattan. Straight ahead led to the much-feared detention rooms.

If you passed all the examinations, the inspectors entered your name in the registry book and gave you a landing card. Of every nine people who received a landing card, three went to New York City. After a twenty-minute ferry ride, they arrived at the tip of Manhattan and began their new lives in America.

The remaining six would buy railroad tickets to other places in the United States. Some went as far as California and Washington State. Others traveled to the midwest, the south, or New England.

Almost everyone had to change their old country's money into American money. The money exchange booth had a sign that said "Bureau of Change" in many different languages. For example, *Cambia Valuta* (Italian), *Zamiana Pieniedzy* (Polish), and *Wechselgeschäft* (German).

If you were going on a long trip, you'd want to buy a box lunch because you couldn't purchase food on the train. For one dollar you could buy a sandwich, fruit, and piece of pie. Like the sign on the money exchange booth, the food was listed in at least three languages: German, Italian, and often Swedish.

Before they left Ellis Island, many people sent telegrams or letters to relatives to tell them when their trains would arrive. Then they went outside to the dock where they boarded ferries to railroad depots in New Jersey. Sometimes their tickets were marked "Special Emigrant ticket," and then they rode in train cars that were for immigrants only. Their new lives in America were about to begin.

Were there any special groups to help immigrants?

There were groups to help almost every nationality. Some religious organizations helped their own members. Other organizations, like the Red Cross, YMCA, Salvation Army, and the Travelers' Aid Society, helped any immigrant, regardless of nationality.

Many groups had representatives at Ellis Island. If a person was detained, often an aid society brought an appeal on his or her behalf. Sometimes these groups distributed crackers and milk for children, and provided box lunches for those traveling on.

Some groups distributed used clothing to the newcomers and searched for missing luggage. The aid groups were also very helpful in locating relatives and friends already in America. In some cases where there were no relatives or friends, the aid group itself helped a new immigrant find work and a place to live.

What impressions did immigrants have of Ellis Island?

Most people were excited by the adventure of coming to a new country. But as they approached Ellis Island, many were nervous and afraid. The place was called "Island of Tears" by many immigrants.

Edward Corsi, who grew up to become Commissioner of Ellis Island, was a child when he came from Italy. He thought, "this could not be a good place," because his mother cried when seeing Ellis Island. She was afraid they might all be sent back.

Some have painful memories of the island. Vera Clark was seven when she came from Barbados. She remembers being herded into a big room. "We were like in cages. . . . There were some of us on one side and some on the other. . . . It was just one human mass of people. Bewildered, black and white, people who weren't speaking English, couldn't understand each other, but all afraid of each other . . . it was just horrible."

Others had happier memories. For some, the great mystery of America was to be found in foods. Lillian Kaiz was seven when she arrived from Russia. "I ate my first hot dog and my first banana there. These were revelations." Lillian had other memories as well. "The first night they were celebrating Christmas. They had a movie. I had never seen one. And there was Santa Claus. And we got tiny little gifts."

George Monezis didn't know his own birthday because he had been born on a Greek island during a period of war and had no birth certificate. On his first day in an American school, his father listed George's birthday as their date of entry at Ellis Island. And so George could never forget his arrival day in America.

Maljan Chavoor summed up his impression in one word. "Jell-O. I fell in love with it. The first time in my life I had Jell-O. I've been eating Jell-O for seventy years since I've been here."

How did people learn English?

Some people have a hard time learning a new language. For others, it's easier.

Some immigrant adults learned English at their jobs, or from neighbors and relatives, or at night school classes. Others never learned, but their children usually did.

In some schools, there were special classes to help students. You'd stay there until you knew enough to go into a regular class. In other schools, there was no special help at all. One young girl from Russia spoke two languages when she arrived — Yiddish and Russian. She stayed in kindergarten until she learned English. She was the first in her family to speak the new language.

A Yugoslavian boy was helped by other kids. During school recess, they'd point at things and repeat the names over and over — button, shoe, eyes, nose, hat, hand. "I used to go home and fall asleep repeating them."

An eleven-year-old from Turkey didn't have such an easy time in school. Some kids teased him and picked fights. "I couldn't read, I couldn't write, I couldn't speak. I had never been to school in my life until I came here, on account of the war over there. But I picked it up. I picked it up very good, thank God."

Did immigrants ever return to "the old country"?

Ever since people first began coming to the United States, some have not wanted to stay. Even in the 1600s, when the colonies were first settled, about one of every six immigrants returned to England, either permanently or temporarily.

Some who came to America never planned to stay. They wanted to earn as much money as they could and then return home to live a better life. Others came as "seasonal workers." They arrived usually in the spring when they could find jobs, and then returned home in winter when the work was finished.

And some simply didn't like it here and went home. They missed their friends and relatives and old way of life. Ethel Suchman felt that way at first. She came as a teenager, lived with relatives in New York City, and after a year decided to go home to Austria. Years later she returned, and this time she stayed for good.

With some nationalities — for example, Italians, Romanians, Slovaks, Greeks — at least twenty percent and sometimes more than half later returned to their old homes. The Irish and the Jews had the fewest people returning. The Irish didn't want to go back to so poor a country. And the Jews, having escaped the pogroms and other discrimination in Russia and eastern Europe, had no safe place to return to.

What did Americans think about the new immigrants?

Although everyone in America is an immigrant or a descendant of an immigrant, there have always been some people who want to keep newcomers out. Others have welcomed them. This has been true for all of American history.

The Declaration of Independence, signed July 4, 1776, created a new nation called the United States of America. In the Declaration, the colonists listed their grievances — what angered them — about King George III and the British parliament. One grievance was that the King had limited immigration to the colonies.

In 1841, President John Tyler invited foreigners "to come and settle among us as members of our rapidly growing family." And President Lincoln described immigrants as "a source of national wealth and strength."

In 1952, President Harry S. Truman vetoed a law that would have let people from northern Europe enter more easily than other immigrants. He said the idea that those with English names "were better people . . . than Americans with Italian or Greek or Polish names . . . is utterly unworthy of our traditions and our ideals."

But a dislike of immigrants began before President Truman. By the mid-1800s, the Know-Nothing Party was a strong anti-immigration political group that believed in keeping out all foreigners. They had begun as a secret society. When anyone asked them about the party, they answered, "I know nothing," and that's how they got their name.

They forgot that their ancestors also had been immigrants. As one historian wrote, they called their relatives who had come in the early years "settlers" or "colonists." Everyone else was an "immigrant."

The Irish and Germans were among the first to be attacked. Job advertisements often read: "No Irish need apply."

There was tremendous prejudice against Asian immigrants — Chinese and Japanese — particularly in California, where most of them had settled. In 1870 the U.S. Congress passed a law that said only white people and people of African descent could become citizens. Then in 1882, the government passed the Chinese Exclusion Act. This law made the Chinese the only group in the world at that time that could not freely come to America. They couldn't become citizens until 1943.

By the end of the nineteenth century, most new immigrants were from southern and eastern Europe. Some groups wanted laws, like the literacy act, passed to keep them out. (See page 48.)

When World War I began, there was a great deal of anti-immigrant feeling in the country. Many people were taken from their homes, sent to Ellis Island, and then deported. After the war, in the 1920s, Congress passed laws that made it very difficult for new immigrants to come to America.

At the time of World War II, America was fighting the Japanese and the Germans. President Roosevelt ordered most Japanese in America to be put in prison areas called internment camps. Even those born in America were rounded up. Nearly fifty years later, Congress recognized that the Japanese internment had been wrong, and the U.S. government agreed to pay those Japanese Americans for the loss of their homes and other property.

Today, thousands of new immigrants are coming to the United States, mostly from Asia and Latin America. These newcomers hope and dream the same dreams as earlier immigrants — a better life for themselves and their children. They are as courageous and as adventurous as the ones who came before them. And like the earlier immigrants, they, too, face discrimination and prejudice as they struggle to become part of what President Tyler called "the American family."

What contributions have immigrants made?

From the time of America's founding, new immigrants have played an important role. Eight of the fifty-five men who signed the Declaration of Independence were born in other countries. And when Thomas Jefferson wrote in the Declaration that "all men are created equal," he used the words of his Italian-born friend Philip Mazzei.

History books often list famous Americans who were immigrants. These lists usually include Albert Einstein, the German-Jewish scientist; Alexander Graham Bell, from Scotland, who invented the telephone; Elizabeth Blackwell, English-born, the first woman doctor in America; Knute Rockne, the Norwegian football player and coach; Marcus Garvey, from Jamaica, the leader of the Back-to-Africa movement; Greta Garbo, the Swedish movie star; Spyros Skouras, the Greek movie producer; Irving Berlin, the Russian-Jewish composer and songwriter; Enrico Fermi, the Italian scientist, and many others.

But millions of immigrants, not just the "famous" ones, created or started things that we think of as totally American. We take these things for granted, but they are the contributions of immigrants:

— log cabins first built by Swedes;

— symphony orchestras and glee clubs organized by Germans;

— movies produced in America by Russian Jews and Greeks;

— Santa Claus, bowling, and ice-skating from the Dutch.

Many peoples contributed to American English. "Yankee" is a Dutch word, and "alligator" is Spanish. "Phooey" is from German, and "prairie" is French. "Jukebox" is African, and "gung ho" is Chinese. And there are hundreds more words that were originally foreign and are now a part of the English language.

If you think of Native American Indians as the first immigrants, then the names of many states come from Indian "immigrant" languages: Arizona, Wisconsin, Wyoming, Connecticut, Mississippi, and Oklahoma, to name a few. "Raccoon," "skunk," and "succotash" also are Indian words.

As Abraham Lincoln said, immigrants have been "a source of national wealth and strength."

Did some immigrants change their names when they came to America?

Many people changed their names or had them changed by an official, like a ship's officer or an Ellis Island inspector. Some immigrants were afraid that they wouldn't be allowed to enter if they had long or unpronounceable names. One young man who came from Russia in 1905 was concerned about his name. So he shortened it from Katznelson to Nelson.

As a child, Nathan Levine learned that his name wasn't really Levine. When his father came to America, he had a long Russian name. The immigration inspectors, Nathan was told, changed many Jewish names to Levine or Cohen. And so his father, Louis Nachimovsky, became Louis Levine.

One woman who worked on Ellis Island for the Hebrew Immigrant Aid Society recalled how inspectors sometimes changed a person's name, often because of a misunderstanding. There is a story about one family that got its name in an unusual way. When a family member arrived in this country, he explained that he was a *yosem*, which means "orphan" in Yiddish. The next thing he knew, his name was listed as Josem.

For many, their new name was the beginning of a new life. They worked very hard, hoping to provide more for their families than they had had as children. Their children became businesspeople, athletes, teachers, doctors, construction workers, artists, lawyers, chefs, writers. The freedom to choose, which brought so many to American shores, was a gift they gave to their children.

When did Ellis Island close?

From 1892 until World War I, Ellis Island was the main port of entry to the United States. Millions passed through the Great Hall and down the Staircase of Separation. Millions made America their new home. When the war began in 1914, ships carrying immigrants stopped crossing the ocean. With the end of the war four years later, immigrants began arriving again.

But within a few years of the war's end, Congress passed laws that severely limited the number of people who were allowed to enter the United States. It was as if the great gateway to America, although still open, was beginning to creak and rust. Over the next years Ellis Island was used as a detention center for people being deported, a hospital for wounded servicemen, a holding center for prisoners of war, and a Coast Guard station.

Buildings, not used, began to decay. Weeds rapidly spread. In 1954, Ellis Island, the place of so much happiness and so many tears, was finally closed.

In 1965 the island was turned over to the National Park Service. Seventeen years later, workers began to restore the main building to what it had looked like when thousands had passed through its halls daily. In the summer of 1990, Ellis Island reopened as an immigration museum.

At the museum, the Ellis Island story is told on film, tape, and in many exhibits. In the first-floor baggage room you can see the actual steamer trunks, suitcases, and baskets that immigrants brought with them so many years ago. Landing cards, passports, and ships' manifest lists are on exhibit. You can walk up the stairs, as millions of immigrants did, to the Great Hall, and then down the Staircase of Separation.

It is estimated that nearly one out of every two Americans has a relative who passed through Ellis Island.

Outside is a great seawall that lists the names of some immigrant families from Aabrahamson to Zyziak. It is the Ellis Island Wall of Honor, built with the contributions of Americans from many backgrounds.